I0044795

"For far too long, most traditional HR practices have cost companies billions. Thankfully, this book reveals how to turn it all around. *Dirty Little HR Secrets* is essential for leaders who want to tap into the true potential of their workforce and use empathy for a strategic advantage."
— Melissa Donahue, Director of Benefits and HR Compliance at BlueTriton Brands

"One big reveal in *Dirty Little HR Secrets* is the immense cost of ignoring employee well-being. But it doesn't stop there. Almost every page challenges traditional norms while offering solutions and new perspectives. This book is a must-read for those ready to transform their workplace into a hub of innovation and loyalty."
— Molly Belmont, Employee Benefits Consultant at Gallagher

"Read *Dirty Little HR Secrets* so you can discover how to transform systemic HR challenges into opportunities for growth and engagement. This book offers a fresh perspective on leadership and management and tools to empower their workforce and harness the benefits of a truly engaged team."
— Jessica Lipson, VP of HR at SEG

"*Dirty Little HR Secrets* isn't just a good read; it's a revolution, offering a blueprint for leaders and CEOs to cultivate a thriving workplace where every employee

feels valued. It's a smart tool for a future where engagement and well-being are not perks but the foundation of every business strategy."
— Jaime Broderick, Business Leadership and Positioning Consultant for High Achieving Entrepreneurs and Corporate Department Heads

"*Dirty Little HR Secrets* is a clarion call to CEOs and leaders. It's a vivid, compelling guide that shows how transforming HR practices can reignite the human spirit and lead to epic financial benefits. This book will inspire you to act, innovate, and lead with heart."
— Marianne McCafferty, Payroll and Retirement

"Clear and direct, this book reveals the profound impact and cost of disengagement and maps out a strategy for cultural change. CEOS and leaders will find a compelling case for embedding empathy and innovation, making them an indispensable part of their organizational culture."
— Dr. Deolinda Reverendo, Dental Practice Partner

"Here's an essential tool for leaders who make impactful changes in their organizations. This book is a masterclass in HR transformation, taking you from the stark revelations of the costs of traditional practices to the immense benefits of a human-centric approach. Everyone should read *Dirty Little HR Secrets*."
— Joe Leary, HR Leader

"*Dirty Little HR Secrets* is a roadmap for leaders who see the benefit, want to do what's right, and are ready to enhance employee engagement and well-being, something that is sorely missed in most organizations."
— John Chain, Area Vice President at Gallagher

A QUICK HELLO

Hi, it's Dawn.

Creating a healthy work culture is essential for any organization aiming to thrive in today's competitive business environment. It's about more than just providing a pleasant workplace; it's about fostering an environment where employees feel valued, respected, and motivated. It's also about understanding the real reasons behind employee turnover.

This book is designed to guide you, whether you are a seasoned leader, a newcomer to human resources, or someone who is simply fed up with a toxic work atmosphere.

In other words, *Dirty Little HR Secrets* is for anyone seeking a profitable, sustainable, human-centric culture of high-quality, loyal employees and teams.

I'm glad you're here.

Turnover damages engagement and makes retention difficult—especially because it costs 50–200 percent of a salary to replace an employee, not to mention the time, loss of institutional wisdom, and so much more.

One of the most important ways to create and maintain a healthy work culture is to have real dialogue about difficult subjects that come up in the workplace.

(Another is to embrace your skeletons, which you'll discover later in the book.)

It's a pleasure to support you. Thank you for helping make workplaces better.

Sincerely,

Dawn Ellery

DIRTY LITTLE HR SECRETS

WHY COMPANIES ARE LOSING BILLIONS ON EMPLOYEE ENGAGEMENT AND HOW YOU CAN TURN IT AROUND

DAWN ELLERY

DIRTY LITTLE HR SECRETS

Why Companies Are Losing Billions on Employee Engagement
And How YOU Can Turn it Around

Copyright © 2024 Sweet Escape, LLC
ALL RIGHTS RESERVED

ISBN: 979-8-89079-150-4 (hardcover)
ISBN: 979-8-89079-151-1 (paperback)
ISBN: 979-8-89079-152-8 (ebook)

No part of this material or its associated ancillary materials may be reproduced or transmitted in any form or by any means, electronic or mechanical, including photocopying, recording, or by any informational storage or retrieval system, without permission from the publisher. For permission requests, contact Sweet Escape **at dawnellery.com.**

Legal and Earnings Disclaimer

While all attempts have been made to verify the information provided in these materials and its ancillary materials, neither the author nor publisher assumes any responsibility for errors, inaccuracies, or omissions and is not responsible for any financial loss by the customer in any manner. Any slights of people or organizations are unintentional. If advice concerning legal or related matters is needed, the services of a qualified professional should be sought. The information contained in these materials is strictly for educational purposes. Therefore, if you wish to apply the ideas contained in these materials, you are taking full responsibility for your actions. Neither the author nor publisher purport these materials as a "get rich scheme," and there is no guarantee, express or implied, that you will earn any money using the strategies, concepts, techniques, and ideas in these materials. Earning potential is entirely dependent on the efforts and skills of the person applying all or part of the strategies, concepts, techniques, and ideas contained in these course materials. Any examples, stories, or case studies are for illustrative purposes only and should not be interpreted as examples of what consumers can generally expect from these materials. No representations in any part of these materials are promises for actual performance. Any statements and strategies offered in these materials are simply opinion or experience and, thus, should not be misinterpreted as promises, results, or guarantees (express or implied).

This material and its associated ancillary materials are not intended for use as a source of professional financial, accounting, legal, personal, or medical advice. You should be aware of the various laws governing business transactions or other business practices in your particular geographical location. The author and publisher disclaim any warranties (express or implied), merchantability, or fitness for any particular purpose. The author and publisher (Sweet Escape) or any of Dawn Ellery's representatives shall in no way, event, or under any circumstances be held liable to any party (or any third party) for any direct, indirect, punitive, special, incidental, or other consequential damages arising directly or indirectly from any use of this material, which is provided "as is," and without warranties.

Dedication

To Derricko, Saxon, and Sasha, thank you for showing me what love is.

TABLE OF CONTENTS

FOREWORD

Who doesn't love dirty little secrets?

They can be exciting, titillating, and spice up your day.

However, when they're infesting the business world, that's a whole other story.

That's why this book is so important.

We live in a world where the relentless pursuit of profit too often destroys the human spirit, not to mention the world in which we live.

I should know.

Before I launched my book coaching and publishing business, I spent almost 30 years working for an array of organizations, mostly for-profit and a handful of nonprofits.

No matter the company, vision, or mission, most employees were treated as expendable, third-class citizens (which drove me out the door).

It's still happening and has to stop.

That's why I was so excited when Dawn came to me and said, "Ben, too many people are suffering at work. This has to change. I need to write a book about it!"

Thankfully, *Dirty Little HR Secrets* is the answer. And it holds the keys that will save companies billions of dollars each year while opening the doors to the "whole person" coming to work.

This book isn't just a call to action; it's a simple, logical, human-centric roadmap for revolutionizing culture and eliminating "traditional" HR practices. It's written for leaders, managers, CEOs, and executives like you, who hold the power to reshape the future.

As you turn the pages, you will discover the mind-blowing costs of neglected employee engagement—not just in dollars lost but in destroyed human potential. This book is a strategic challenge to the status quo, inviting a departure from archaic thinking practices that have led organizations to bleed innovation and talent at an alarming rate.

Imagine a workplace where everyone feels valued—not as cogs in a machine but as human beings with unique contributions. If you think this isn't possible (with respect), you're completely wrong. Through a blend of Ellery's hard-earned wisdom, penetrating insights, and actionable strategies, this book equips you to create a cultural renaissance in your organization.

It dares you to build a workplace of empathy and innovation, where employee well-being is not just a policy but a cornerstone of your strategy.

This book isn't just about employee engagement and well-being; it's about reigniting human potential and transforming workplaces into environments where creativity flourishes, loyalty deepens, and goals and objectives are met with enthusiasm and commitment.

If you're ready to lead courageously and embrace a future of putting your people first, *Dirty Little HR Secrets* is your manifesto. It not only illustrates (sometimes painfully) what is going wrong but also illuminates the path to what we can do right—together.

As you take the journey through this book, remember that change starts with awareness and comes to life with action. I invite you to let this book be your guide to creating a legacy of leadership that values, supports, and empowers the lifeblood of your organization.

It's not just an investment in your organization's future but in the future of the people who make your company what it is.

Welcome to the new era of human-centric leadership.

Welcome to *Dirty Little HR Secrets*.

Thanks for being here!

— Ben Gioia, Book Coach and Publisher,
CEO of Leadership Awake, LLC,
Creator of The Influence With A Heart® Method

1

UNLOCKING THE SECRETS TO SAVING BILLIONS IN HR COSTS

All companies want better employee engagement because better engagement means better retention, which leads to lower costs, a human-centered culture, better customer experience, and a brand that magnetically attracts the right clients, customers, partners, investors, and stakeholders.

However, almost everything they're doing is wrong.

Did you know that companies are losing an estimated $600 billion per year because of:

1. The lack of employee engagement
2. The cost of ineffective programs that try to fix the symptoms but don't solve the underlying problems of disengagement

The global levels of employee engagement have hovered at a low 20 percent since engagement started being tracked.

In the US, the number is at a low 30 percent.

Nothing companies are doing has made a significant impact.

HR INSANITY

HR insanity is doing the same thing (on repeat) while expecting engagement, retention, profitability, and success.

I should know because I've witnessed it (and experienced it).

Even as a deeply empathic person, I've "survived" HR.

I've spent 25 years working in human resources departments, and I've been disengaged the whole time. While the decision-makers thought they were positively changing the work culture by adding reward and recognition programs, they were only maintaining the status quo.

My experience is not unique. Only 27 percent of workers worldwide say they have a healthy relationship to work (Business Insider – survey 15,000).

And a whopping 83 percent of people would take a pay cut to be happier at work!

This begs the question: "What can we do to make employees happier?"

Dirty Little HR Secrets is a great place to start.

In the pages of this book, you'll discover an array of real, actionable solutions (that save companies billions of dollars worldwide).

The most profound conversations about life, love, and personal happiness often take place in the most unexpected settings.

- If you're a leader/CHRO or director of total rewards, you'll discover how to positively impact your employees' lives, leading to increased productivity and a better customer experience.
- If you're an HR professional, you'll discover how to elevate employee engagement in ways outside of traditional rewards and recognition programs.
- If you're a disengaged employee, you'll be surprised by some things your employer could do to make you a little more engaged at work.

There is lots of opportunity and some work to be done.

HEALTHY CULTURE CANNOT BE BUILT OVERNIGHT

One common myth is that a healthy culture can be built overnight. Another misconception is that a fun office space equates to a healthy culture.

While a vibrant office can contribute to a positive environment, the underlying values, communication, and leadership truly define the culture.

Investing in employee development is another key aspect.

Finally, it's important to lead by example. As a leader, your actions set the tone for the entire organization. By embodying the values you want to see, you inspire others to follow suit.

Building a healthy work culture is a multifaceted endeavor that requires dedication and a strategic approach. By debunking common myths and focusing on effective communication, recognition, employee development, and leading by example, you can create an environment where everyone feels empowered to contribute their best.

You may save your organization millions (if not billions) of dollars by doing a few things differently. It's all about engagement, retention, productivity, and well-being.

I'm glad you're here. Thanks for your willingness to create a better workplace.

(You may not know this, but the key to billion-dollar workplaces came from my experience as an entrepreneur opening and running a sex shop for almost five years—more on this later.)

WHO THIS BOOK IS FOR

This book is for leaders, managers, CEOs, and executives—like you—who hold the power to reshape the future.

In the seemingly eternal (yet short-sighted) quest for "the bottom line," most businesses have spent decades (if not centuries) excluding mental well-being from the workplace.

When I say mental well-being, I mean emotions, personality, whole-beingness, and individuality.

In reality, mental well-being is a polite way of addressing the real issue: the mental health crisis that's been created and amplified by most businesses around the world.

According to the US Surgeon General, 76 percent of US workers reported at least one symptom of a mental health condition, and 84 percent say their workplace conditions have contributed to at least one mental health challenge.

The good news is that corporations are beginning to take notice and act. The bad news is that most of them are moving way too slowly to affect any significant change.

It's not surprising because of entrenched and habitual thinking, plus a lack of empathy that continues to put profits before people.

At the same time, employees are calling for support and healthy work environments, with 81 percent of them saying they will be looking for workplaces that support mental health in the future.

- That's a retention killer right there.
- Plus, a huge loss of talent and wisdom.
- Not to mention the global price tag of billions of dollars.

So, this book isn't just about employee engagement and well-being; it's about reigniting human potential. It's about transforming workplaces into environments where creativity flourishes, loyalty deepens, and goals and objectives are met with enthusiasm and commitment.

WHY MOST EMPLOYEE ENGAGEMENT PROGRAMS DON'T WORK

As we get started on this adventure together, here are three important definitions:

1. **Employee Engagement:** The connection between an employee base who wants to be doing what they are doing, feels valued and seen, and buys into the mission of an organization to increase their productivity.
2. **Employee Well-being:** The overall state of an employee's physical, mental, financial, and emotional health. It includes factors such as job satisfaction, work-life balance, and feeling supported and valued in the workplace. High employee well-being leads to increased productivity, engagement, and resilience, benefiting both the individual and the organization.
3. **Employee Mental Well-being:** The state of an employee's emotional, psychological, and social health at work. It encompasses the ability to handle stress, maintain positive relationships, stay resilient, and feel fulfilled, supported, and valued in their role. A high level of mental well-being enables employees to thrive personally and professionally, contributing positively to their team and the organization.

I wanted to call out mental well-being and define it because it is a focal point of my story and what I believe to be a cornerstone of employee engagement.

Enhancing employee engagement and well-being is not just a noble endeavor; it's a necessity for any organization aiming to thrive. Employee engagement and well-being are intertwined, with each influencing the other. Engagement is about employees feeling connected to their work and the organization's mission, while well-being encompasses their physical, mental, emotional, and financial health.

Unfortunately, despite increased awareness, many companies still struggle to improve these crucial aspects. Traditional corporate cultures often pressure employees to appear perpetually okay, suppressing their authentic selves and any issues that don't fit within narrow parameters.

This expectation to leave one's personal life at the door, combined with outdated leadership views, creates an environment where it's challenging for managers to recognize when employees need support.

The reality is that employees are not expendable; they are the backbone of any organization. With mental health issues on the rise and physical health concerns, such as obesity, becoming more common, it's clear that behaviors significantly impact well-being. Yet, there seems to be a collective reluctance to address these issues openly and make the necessary lifestyle changes.

To break this cycle and foster a culture of genuine engagement and well-being, honesty and vulnerability must be encouraged.

It's okay *not* to be okay.

For organizations to thrive, it's critical to provide support that acknowledges the individuality of each employee, moving beyond one-size-fits-all solutions. Before even considering implementing rewards and recognition programs, it's crucial to address the root causes of disengagement.

In a nutshell, *all business decisions are personal.*

Organizations can reverse the declining engagement and well-being by creating an environment where employees feel valued, supported, and encouraged to be their authentic selves. This shift not only benefits the employees but also leads to increased productivity, innovation, and overall success for the business.

Who I Am and Why It Matters

One way I'm seen in the world is as an HR leader.

Today, I have a role I love in a company that's an absolute pleasure to be a part of, but it wasn't always like this.

I've spent a great deal of my life feeling unseen, as if I didn't fit in. I felt forced to wear a costume or mask to fit into other people's expectations—all to make a living in the corporate world.

What I hadn't felt all those years was engaged, appreciated, and heard (seen) in my work. I consider myself a disengaged high performer. I was aware years ago that my chosen field was not my passion, but when I start something, I dive in and become the best I can.

It's taken me time to embrace the authentic me, find my passions, and start to use them in engaging, fulfilling, and purposeful work. It's been a long road of suffering, avoiding, then confronting, and finally healing.

Having spent the better part of the last 25 years in the above toxic environment had me constantly wondering why things had to be done "this" way. *What is wrong with me? Why can't I just do my job, collect my paycheck, and live a happy life?*

I'm good at my job but have needed to put up a false front so leaders were comfortable hiring me. I found that being good at something and being able to make a large salary while doing it did not lead to—or was not a substitute for—the happiness and well-being I was searching for.

I have always been the proponent of the under-dog, and that is typically the employee within the corporate world. Human resources are typically the risk mitigators for the company and do not always make decisions that serve the welfare of the employees as a primary focus.

For years, I've brought team members into toxic and unhealthy work environments. I acted like everything was fine and that I was happy and content in my role within the company.

The environment was not healthy, so I solved my problem by moving companies. It was a continual short-term solution.

I was fooled during countless interviews into believing that this job or this company would be the environment where I would feel safe, supported, and nurtured so I could bring my best to the organization.

I didn't find this until I embraced my skeletons (more on this later in the book).

The corporate work environment has left me angry and a little sad that I'd remained on this same treadmill (minus my four-year entrepreneurial stint) without raising my voice sooner.

So now, I have chosen to help current and future generations of employees and leaders create a healthier and more supportive work environment.

The how, where, and when of hitting rock bottom and how I turned everything around may come as quite a shock, as you'll see later in this book.

If you're ready for some support, feel free to reach out to me for a conversation at dawn@dawnellery.com or linkedin.com/in/dawnellery. I look forward to meeting you!

Why Traditional HR Strategies Fail and What to Do Instead

During the pandemic, my career took a pivotal turn as I delved into coaching, pushing me to scrutinize the efficacy of conventional HR practices, particularly around performance management. This exploration opened the door to one-on-one wellness coaching within the workplace, a method distinctively not centered solely on job performance metrics. Through these sessions, I stumbled upon profound insights that would reshape my understanding of workplace dynamics.

Among the employees I coached, two stood out due to their notable struggles at work. These individuals, previously overlooked for additional support, were teetering on the edge of being placed on a performance improvement plan (PIP), yet as I engaged more deeply with them, a different story began to unfold—one not of incompetence or lack of knowledge but of personal turmoil profoundly impacting their professional lives.

Take, for instance, one employee who was navigating the stormy waters of divorce from an emotionally abusive relationship. The personal bravery required to make such a life-altering decision spilled over into his work life, causing a disconnect with the company's mission. This disconnection wasn't born from dissatisfaction with the job but from a deep transformation in his personal values and goals. He felt a strong pull toward more meaningful, community-focused work, especially in aiding underfunded areas.

This scenario highlighted a critical flaw in traditional HR strategies: They often fail to recognize and address the root causes of employee disengagement, which are frequently personal and deeply emotional. The standard approach would have pushed him further into a system that didn't align with his evolving needs and aspirations, potentially leading to the loss of a valuable employee who simply needed the space and support to realign his professional path.

Through coaching, we facilitated a plan that allowed him to gracefully exit the company, providing him the time he needed to pursue his newfound calling. Simultaneously, this transition period benefited the company by allowing for a seamless handover to a new employee, who could learn from his experience and take over his responsibilities without the usual disruptions of a sudden departure.

This experience underscored the importance of understanding the human element in HR practices and the potential for coaching to bridge the gap between personal development and professional demands, creating a more supportive and adaptive workplace environment.

THE COST OF IGNORING EMPLOYEE MENTAL HEALTH IN THE WORKPLACE

If I hadn't intervened, the employee and his manager would have been on a path toward a performance improvement plan (PIP), a route fraught with frustration and despair that likely would have culminated in the loss of his job, severely impacting his mental well-being. Recognizing the risks, we opted for a different approach: We set up a transition plan, a glide path, which not only helped him exit the role without the stress of immediate job loss but also positioned him for a future where he could pursue work that truly aligned with his values and aspirations.

This strategic shift prevented the high costs typically associated with employee turnover, ranging from 50 to 200 percent of an employee's salary. By planning a thoughtful exit, we allowed for a smooth knowledge transfer to a new hire, preserving organizational knowledge and avoiding the disruptive gaps that often follow an abrupt departure. This method not only saved the company significant potential costs but also supported the employee's journey toward a more fulfilling and engaging career, demonstrating a crucial balance between organizational needs and individual well-being.

HUMAN DEVELOPMENT IS PROFITABLE, SUSTAINABLE, AND GOOD FOR EVERYONE

Imagine stepping into a company where everyone, from the top down, shares the goal of not just growing professionally but also becoming better human beings. This concept stands in stark contrast to the traditional corporate approach to employee development, which often centers primarily on what the organization can gain. Typically, companies analyze the return on investment for the training and development opportunities they provide, focusing on how these initiatives will benefit the company's bottom line.

However, true growth extends beyond just business gains. It's crucial that employee development also considers the personal well-being and growth of each individual. This broader perspective ensures that while the company advances, its employees do, too—not just as workers but as well-rounded individuals. This approach fosters a more supportive and sustainable work environment and creates a win-win scenario where both the company and its employees thrive together.

WIN-WIN-WIN CAREER PROGRESSION STRATEGIES

In the realm of human resources, career ladders are a cornerstone of compensation planning. Traditionally, these ladders are built within the confines of the company, rarely allowing employees the flexibility to grow outside the organizational structure. This internal focus often overlooks the individual's broader career aspirations, which may extend beyond the current workplace.

Imagine if companies reimagined this growth not just as a benefit to the organization but as an attribute of the individual's career journey. What if training programs, career planning, and developmental opportunities were crafted with the understanding that an employee's growth benefits both the individual and the company, even if that path leads them outside the company eventually?

The modern career trajectory is vastly different from the past. Estimates suggest that individuals will hold around 12 different jobs throughout their lives, challenging the outdated notion of lifetime employment at a single company. Yet, many corporate HR policies still cling to the idea of retaining employees indefinitely, designing career paths that assume decades of service within the same organization.

However, fostering a more flexible approach to career progression will benefit both the employee and the company. Allowing employees to experience various roles across different departments or even supporting their growth outside the company can lead to more fulfilled, well-rounded professionals.

This approach acknowledges the reality of modern careers and provides a framework that supports the employee's entire professional journey, enhancing their contributions to the company during their tenure. Such a strategy not only meets the needs of the individual but also adapts to the evolving landscape of the work-force, creating a win-win-win scenario for employees, HR, and the company as a whole.

How To Make Real Change

If you're a leader/CHRO or director of total rewards, you'll see how to get to the root of employee (dis) engagement. You'll discover the most effective ways to impact the lives of your employees in a positive way, which will lead to increased productivity and a better customer experience.

It's a win-win-win.

If you're an HR professional, you'll see how to elevate engagement from outside traditional rewards and recognition programs.

And you may just save your organization millions—if not billions—of dollars by doing a few things differently, with a focus on engagement, retention, productivity, and well-being.

This is not a pipe dream.

These approaches work and will work for you.

(And if you're ready for some support, feel free to reach out to me for a conversation at dawn@dawnellery.com or linkedin.com/in/dawnellery. I look forward to meeting you!)

A Tool You Can Use Today

Giving your managers the opportunity to be more effective and empathic with their employees by giving them tools they may never have been exposed to increases manager engagement. Then, they will have more confidence in their one-on-one conversations and feel prepared for something unexpected.

One little hinge that swings big doors in organizations is navigating difficult conversations.

If you're ready for some support, feel free to reach out to me for a conversation at dawn@dawnellery.com or linkedin.com/in/dawnellery. I look forward to meeting you!

2

EMPLOYEE ENGAGEMENT: THE FIVE BIGGEST MYTHS

L et's take a closer look at the biggest myths and misunderstandings about employee engagement and employee well-being.

The corporate world is notoriously slow to adapt. Decades of entrenched thinking have led to a stagnation in engagement levels, coupled with a decline in mental health and overall human fulfillment.

It's clear that simply throwing money at the problem is not the solution.

It's time to reevaluate the myths and assumptions that have been guiding engagement strategies.

The pursuit of the "purple unicorn" of a highly engaged workforce seems more elusive than ever despite the significant resources devoted to achieving it.

The approach to employee engagement and well-being has long been centered around rewards and recognition programs, underpinned by the belief that a bigger budget leads to better outcomes. Companies are investing billions of dollars into these initiatives, including service awards, employee engagement surveys, recognition programs, and well-being programs.

Despite these hefty investments, studies like Gallup's State of the Global Workplace: 2023 Report reveal a concerning trend: Low engagement is costing the global economy an estimated $8.8 trillion annually due to lost productivity.

BREAKING THE CYCLE OF "HR INSANITY"

This low engagement situation raises critical questions about the effectiveness of current engagement strategies. The conventional wisdom suggests that financial incentives and recognition are key to boosting employee engagement. However, the persistent issue of low global engagement, hovering around 22 percent, flies in the face of this notion.

It's time to move beyond these myths and take meaningful action to make a real impact. This involves rethinking the role of rewards and recognition, understanding the deeper drivers of engagement, and addressing the root causes of disengagement. Companies can pave the way for a more engaged, fulfilled, and productive workforce by challenging the status quo and adopting a more holistic approach.

When you bring clear awareness to a situation, you can then make choices that are win-win-win (for companies, employees, and the public).

Unraveling the myths surrounding employee engagement and well-being is crucial for making informed decisions that benefit everyone involved. By shining the light on these misconceptions, you can pave the way for a more holistic and effective approach to fostering a positive work environment.

THE FIVE BIGGEST MYTHS

Myth #1: My employees' happiness is not my concern.

REALITY: Employee happiness is directly linked to productivity and customer satisfaction. Employees who feel content and valued are more likely to go the extra mile for your company and your clients. It's essential to recognize that the well-being of your employees is a vital component of your business's success.

Myth #2: An employee engagement survey needs to be part of your employee engagement strategy.

REALITY: While surveys can provide insights, they are not the be-all and end-all of engagement strategies. The key is to make sure the feedback you receive is genuine and reflective of your employees' true sentiments. Relying solely on survey results without considering other factors can lead to misguided efforts that fail to address the real issues.

Myth #3: Manager training is not a necessity.

REALITY: Effective management is not an innate skill; it requires training and development. The relationship between employees and their managers is a critical factor in engagement and well-being. Investing in manager training can equip your leaders with the tools they need to foster a supportive and motivating work environment.

Myth #4: Having a medical plan and an employee assistance program (EAP) provides all the mental health support employees need.

REALITY: While these resources are important, they are not sufficient on their own. Access to mental health care is often challenging, and EAPs typically have low utilization rates. It's important to actively promote these programs and explore additional ways to support your employees' mental health.

Myth #5: Engagement can be solved by implementing a rewards and recognition program.

REALITY: Rewards and recognition are important, but they can't fix engagement issues on their own. True engagement comes from a deeper connection to the work and the organization. It's about creating an environment where employees feel heard, respected, and aligned with the company's values and goals.

Now that we've dug into the myths a bit, allow me to share how I help organizations transform systemic HR challenges into opportunities for growth, engagement, and more.

THE EMPLOYEE ENGAGEMENT R.E.S.E.T. (SNAPSHOT)

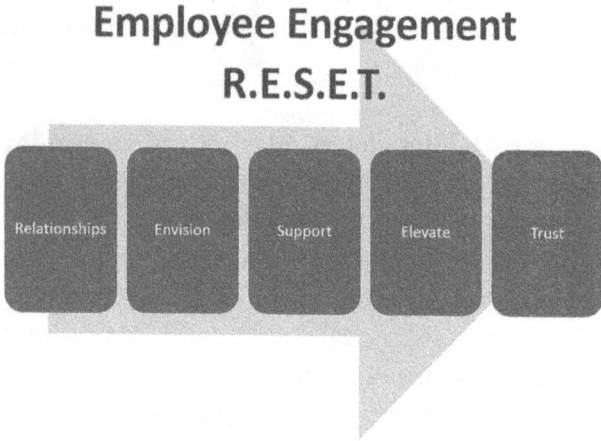

Employee Engagement
R.E.S.E.T.

Relationships   Envision   Support   Elevate   Trust

The Employee Engagement R.E.S.E.T. is the key to unlocking a more engaged, productive, profitable, and fulfilling workplace. It's a simple yet comprehensive approach that challenges conventional wisdom and seeks to address the foundational aspects of employee engagement.

While we'll be digging deeper later in the book, here's a snapshot of the R.E.S.E.T. to get you started.

When I'm consulting for organizations, running workshops, or speaking from a stage, I like to use a simple acronym—R.E.S.E.T.—because it's easy to remember and helps keep organizations on track.

Part 1 – RELATIONSHIPS: It's As Easy As ABC

The relationship between employees and their managers is the cornerstone of engagement. A healthy relationship fosters trust, open communication, and a sense of belonging. Similarly, a positive team culture encourages collaboration, respect, and mutual support. Both are essential for creating an environment where employees feel motivated and engaged.

Part 2 – ENVISION: Reimagining HR

If employees don't feel they are growing personally and professionally, they may quit tomorrow. Opportunities for development and advancement are crucial. Equally important is a sense of belonging. Employees should feel that they are an integral part of the organization and that their contributions are valued.

Part 3 – SUPPORT: Compensation Won't Solve For Engagement

Compensation and benefits are important, but they are not the only factors that contribute to employee well-being and engagement. Organizations need to provide support and resources that address all aspects of an employee's well-being.

Part 4 – ELEVATE: Profiting by Putting People First

It's critical for the values, mission, and goals of the organization to align with those of its employees. When employees feel that their work is meaningful and contributes to a larger purpose, they are more likely to be engaged and committed to the organization.

Part 5 – TRUST: Communication That Transforms

Effective communication is the thread that ties all the other elements together.

Communication is interwoven throughout the foundation and across all stages of growth for an organization.

ESSENTIAL STEPS TO CULTIVATE A HUMAN-CENTERED CORPORATE CULTURE

The most important takeaway from the Employee Engagement R.E.S.E.T. is that engagement is a multifaceted issue that requires a holistic solution.

There is really no separation between one's work life and one's home life. And all business decisions are indeed personal.

By focusing on the foundational aspects of the employee experience, organizations can create an environment where engagement can thrive. By doing so, organizations both improve engagement and enhance the overall well-being and productivity of their workforce.

DOES YOUR ORGANIZATION NEED A R.E.S.E.T?

Ready for an Employee Engagement R.E.S.E.T now? Do you want to cultivate a human-centered corporate culture that's profitable and sustainable?

Connect with me today at linkedin.com/in/dawnellery or email me directly at dawn@dawnellery.com.

I look forward to speaking with you soon!

EMBRACING YOUR SKELETONS

As I shared earlier, there is really no separation between one's work life and one's home life. And all business decisions are indeed personal.

Recognizing that personal histories influence professional behaviors can lead you to foster a supportive environment that addresses these underlying issues.

The root of many workplace engagement issues can be traced back to personal experiences and unresolved emotional conflicts (often from as far back as childhood). Known as adverse childhood experiences (ACEs), these events shape how individuals perceive and react to challenges throughout their lives. Understanding this can be a game-changer for you as a leader.

However, it gets tricky when it comes to talking about it because difficult conversations are often avoided in both personal and professional settings.

Almost 70 percent of employees avoid difficult conversations at work, and over half of employees handle toxic situations by ignoring them. This avoidance can lead to a build-up of misunderstandings and resentment, and these issues can significantly impact employee engagement in any workplace. Recognizing and addressing the discomfort of these conversations is essential for improving communication and strengthening relationships within your company.

Many people stay in uncomfortable or unhappy situations simply because it feels safer than facing the unknown. On average, employees remain with toxic bosses for seven years and with supportive bosses for five years.

This mindset can be particularly harmful in a business environment, where it stifles growth and innovation. As a business leader, encouraging open dialogue and confronting issues directly can pave the way for a more dynamic and responsive organizational culture.

Mental well-being is not just a personal issue but a crucial component of a profitable business strategy. SHRM research cites that one in three employees say that their mental health is negatively impacted by their jobs. Companies that prioritize the mental health of their employees can differentiate themselves and outperform their competitors. This approach involves not only recognizing the signs of distress and offering support but also creating a work environment that actively promotes psychological well-being.

A compassionate and comprehensive approach is key to effectively addressing these challenges. This involves creating policies that support mental health, providing resources for personal development, and fostering a workplace culture that recognizes the value of every employee. By integrating these practices, you can help your team break free from unproductive patterns and move toward a healthier, more engaged, and more fulfilling professional life.

Knowing how to navigate difficult conversations is a game-changer.

(And here's something you've probably never heard: The biggest parallel I've experienced between the corporate workplace and operating a sex shop is difficult conversations—more on this soon.)

What are your thoughts and insights?

_____

_____

_____

_____

_____

_____

_____

_____

_____

_____

_____

_____

_____

_____

_____

Sex Shop Wisdom Solves Big Corporate Challenges (My Story)

Today, I'm honored and blessed to be a successful HR leader, coach, and speaker, and it's a joy to help organizations make their workplace better for everyone.

But it wasn't always like this.

As I mentioned before, the how, where, and when of hitting rock bottom and then pressing my R.E.S.E.T. to turn everything around may come as quite a shock.

Back then, standing in my office with actual walls that allowed for privacy instead of the open space and clear walls we now furnish offices with, I'd stare out the window, trapped in what I thought was my dream job. It was year three at this organization, and I was teetering on the edge of my first severe depression.

Every day felt heavier with the burden of a paycheck that seemed to anchor me deeper into my despair. At home, my kids played under the watchful eyes of their stay-at-home dad, oblivious to the turmoil their mother was facing.

In those days, the only person who truly understood the depth of my struggles was Karen, a wellness coach from work. We had grown close during the lengthy commutes for a company wellness program we were launching.

I vividly remember the heartache of sitting in her car at a train station, sobbing uncontrollably, as she urged me to open up to my husband about my struggles. But before I could take that step, my professional world crumbled; I lost my job over office politics, a betrayal by someone I had considered a friend.

Reeling from the shock and stained by the feeling of failure, I threw myself into job interviews for HR positions. It was all I knew and the only way I believed I could support my family. Yet, with each interview, I felt more disconnected, inadvertently sabotaging my chances by being overly personal or mentioning my children too often.

I was lost, unsure of my next move, until an episode of Oprah changed everything. She featured a sex shop on her show, and something about the lighthearted, inviting atmosphere sparked an interest in me—a stark contrast to the gloomy world of HR in which I was entangled.

Deeply curious and with a desperate need for change, I proposed the idea to my husband. His skepticism was palpable, grounded in the realities of our life—two young children and his role as their primary caretaker. Nevertheless, six months later, we opened Sweet Escape, an intimacy boutique in New Hope, Pennsylvania.

The transition from HR executive to sex shop owner raised eyebrows and fueled endless questions about my drastic career change. Initially, my explanations were superficial: I was unhappy in HR, and starting the boutique seemed like fun after hitting rock bottom.

However, the true transformation began one busy Saturday night at the store. Derrick and I were working together for one of the rare times since opening. The interaction with customers discussing products that were usually taboo in day-to-day conversation revealed a new side of me. Derrick's offhand comment about the interaction being "hot" sparked a cascade of realizations. I had never been open about my desires—not even with my husband.

The store became a place of discovery, not just for our customers but for me as well. I realized that I had never truly asked myself what I wanted in life, always conforming to others' expectations instead of exploring my desires.

This journey of self-discovery highlighted a stark reality: The most profound conversations about life, love, and personal happiness often take place in the most unexpected settings. At Sweet Escape, I facilitated discussions that most avoid at all costs—conversations about intimacy and personal satisfaction. This mirrored the avoidance I had witnessed in corporate HR, where employees suffered silently in jobs that drained their spirits.

The lesson was clear and one that I am now committed to sharing: Real growth and fulfillment come from facing uncomfortable truths and engaging in difficult conversations.

This principle holds true whether in a boutique discussing personal desires or in an office setting addressing career fulfillment.

The support and authenticity I found in the entrepreneurial world taught me that understanding and addressing personal needs is crucial, a lesson that the rigid corporate environment rarely accommodates. Now, I bring this openness and authenticity back into the corporate sphere, advocating for environments where honest conversations can lead to genuine satisfaction and success.

3

THE EMPLOYEE ENGAGEMENT R.E.S.E.T. IN ACTION

Employee Engagement R.E.S.E.T.

Relationships — Envision — Support — Elevate — Trust

SUMMARY

When you're building anything from a business to a relationship, there must be a strong foundation. Without a strong foundation, cracks, slides, and full destruction are ongoing possibilities. You'll see how organizations can begin to shore up their foundations.

This isn't found in company values or mission statements; it is more basic than that. The foundation of any organization is its people. For the foundation to be solid, the people who make up the organization need to be nurtured and supported within their roles and beyond.

In a rapidly evolving business landscape, it can be tempting for companies to focus solely on high returns and quick growth. However, the most resilient and profitable organizations have something crucial in common: They build from a strong foundation rooted in employee well-being. When organizations genuinely prioritize the needs, aspirations, and overall health of their workforce, they unlock engagement levels that cannot be replicated through perks or incentives alone.

A well-supported workforce feels valued and empowered to bring their best selves to work, increasing not only productivity but also retention. Employees who see their company investing in their well-being are more likely to view themselves as integral parts of the organization's mission—an indispensable status that drives loyalty, creativity, and long-term commitment. This foundation doesn't only benefit the workforce; it amplifies the company's bottom line. Studies consistently show that companies with engaged, well-cared-for employees outperform those without such investment in metrics like profitability, customer satisfaction, and innovation.

Building on this foundation aligns with one of the core principles of a successful business: To thrive, an organization must cultivate an environment where employees feel not just present but essential.

R.E.S.E.T. Factor 1 – Relationships: They're As Easy As ABC

The relationships among employees and their managers are a cornerstone of engagement. A healthy relationship fosters trust, open communication, and a sense of belonging. Similarly, a positive team culture encourages collaboration, respect, and mutual support. Both are essential for creating an environment where employees feel motivated and engaged. The foundation is all about employee-manager relationships and team culture.

People Leave Managers, Not Companies

Even though everybody knows this:

- The expertise of managers is left to chance.
- The competence of managers is left to chance.
- The manager-employee relationship is left to chance.

The employee-manager relationship can be even more impactful to someone's well-being than a spouse, a therapist, or their doctor. Research and studies prove this again and again.

After finishing this chapter, you will have tools to show managers another avenue than solely relying on performance management to assist their teams. These new tools will create greater support for employees and better dynamics between managers and employees.

Here's a common situation that most in HR and leadership have faced.

A manager comes to your office wanting to fire someone.

First Question: "What's going on?"

Manager's Answer: "I need to get rid of Mary. I can't take this anymore. She's not doing her job, and things just imploded with a customer. My whole team looks bad because of her."

The HR professional will want to understand what conversations you've had with Mary and what her performance reviews look like.

Manager's Answer: "Well, I haven't really spoken to Mary about this yet. I wanted to get guidance from you first. All of Mary's reviews have been fine. I didn't want to impact her by giving her a poor rating on her annual review."

If you work in HR, you know this story because, unfortunately, it happens all the time. You may also know this story from the manager's point of view. I will confess that I do.

The interesting part of this conundrum is that it typically stems from positive intentions.

When a small issue or performance blip comes up, we give the person a pass, thinking they might be having a hard day or something's going on that they're distracted by. You would want the same consideration, so you give it to others.

- You give the employee a pass and figure this is just a one-time bump.

Sometimes, this is just one or two times, and then the employee is back on track. However, sometimes, it lasts longer and starts impacting broader areas that pull negative attention to your department or team.

- You become annoyed but avoid a difficult conversation and ask them to redo things—maybe via a passive-aggressive email exchange.

OR

- You do it yourself, completely avoiding any interaction with your employee.

I can speak to this turn of events from both the manager's and HR's point of view.

I've given people I manage a pass on performance issues because I figured they had a bad day or were going through something. I swept it aside and didn't want to invade someone's privacy.

Their performance did not improve.

Soon, I had an underperforming employee I was having conversations with who finally confided in me that he had been going through a bitter divorce, and concentration and attention to detail were not happening.

I worked with this employee to manage expectations, and together, we created a plan moving forward that supported the employee and maintained the level of accuracy and workload for the department.

I soon realized that ignoring the performance issue and just giving a pass to the employee didn't help the employee and didn't help our team in the long run.

I started seeing performance issues as a cry for help. This led to the creation of "The ABCs of Relationships – Leading with Care: Promoting Mental Health Awareness and Solutions for Managers" to help managers support employees from the outset of a problem instead of avoiding difficult conversations and waiting for the only course of action available to be managing someone out of the organization.

When Do Employees Need Support? It's as Easy as ABC

Here are six steps to guide managers toward a fresh approach to handling performance issues and gaining insight into their employees' perspectives. Remind managers of these options and of the support they will have from the organization when applying them.

1. **A**ssess the relationship.
2. **B**e open to noticing signs.
3. **C**hallenge your frame of mind.
4. **A**cknowledge your limits.
5. Know the **B**enefits.
6. Keep **C**ommunicating.

When I train managers within organizations on "Leading with Care: Promoting Mental Health Awareness and Solutions for Managers," they find themselves with the skills to notice and identify when disengagement or changes in work performance are about support and communication more than they are about actual performance.

Now, let's break down each of the six steps and see what's inside.

STEP 1: ASSESS THE RELATIONSHIP

I've had people tell me that I don't have to like someone to work with them. That has not worked well for me either as a manager or an employee.

We don't have to be BFFs, but I do need to like and respect the people I am directly working with for more than 30 percent of each day. For me, this entails my direct boss, the team I manage, and those in similar-level positions in our department.

If there is not a healthy relationship on both sides of the employee-manager equation, engagement is hard, if not impossible, to cultivate. You can throw money, raises, and bonuses at employees and give them points through your rewards and recognition programs, and you will still not engage someone who has a poor relationship with their boss or one of their team members.

The strength of the team dynamics of a department is only as strong as the dynamic of the leaders within the department. If you're losing people in one department or work site, it is not just the immediate manager; it may not even be directly about them.

You have to go all the way to the senior leaders to understand the dynamic being created.

To those who have told me that I don't have to like someone to work with them and then forced me or a teammate to work in an unhealthy and even toxic environment to the detriment of the people and the organization, I ask, "Why?"

You're not looking for best friends, but relationships where one person has power demand a level of trust.

Setting expectations for your relationships is crucial. Understanding where your relationship currently stands with each of your team members is a great place to start.

How do you find this out?

- Individual or group coaching.
- Ask each person on your team to complete an anonymous survey: 360 Review for you.
- One-on-one will only work if your employees are honest, which is hard to discern.

These can be difficult conversations when you have an unhealthy relationship in the workplace. Moving past unhealthy relationships involves getting feedback to understand where the relationship sits now and then doing something with that information to build a foundation for a healthy relationship.

What questions should a manager ask their employees to get to know them and help support a healthy relationship? Ask open-ended questions that help you understand what motivates your employees:

- What do you want out of life or at least your time with this company and from me as a manager?
- Where do you want to be in a few years? In ten years? (The answer should not always be at your company.)
- What skills do you want to acquire while working here? (This is an ongoing question.)

- What are your areas of interest that I could support you in, find training for you, or be aware of?

You want the conversation to be about how the manager will support the employee in ways that are in line with the employee's goals.

Where do the company goals fit in? You will find the answer to how personal goals and company goals align within the company phase of your R.E.S.E.T.

SELF-AWARENESS

One of the reasons we need to assess relationship status is that people interpret things differently due to their experiences. Too many of us are completely unaware of the impact of our words and actions on others.

Since it is common in the workplace to always act as if everything is okay, it has become very difficult to know if someone is upset.

People are not always aware of their emotions, and how they express their emotions impacts others. Ninety to ninety-five percent of us believe we are self-aware.

In reality, only 10 to 15 percent of us are estimated to be self-aware.

The un-self-awareness of a leader can cut a team's chance of success in half.

Once someone is past the stage of being a new manager, skills, competency, and impact on team members are not paid attention to by senior leadership and those hiring the manager into a new company. It becomes an assumption that the new manager coming in will gel with the team, peers, and boss, with only a few interviews used to gain this perspective.

This expectation that you are spending 30 percent of your time with people you may have met a couple of times, and some you may never have met before starting a new job, leaves too much room for unhealthy relationships to grow starting from day one.

AGAIN, EMBRACING YOUR SKELETONS

I had one leader who was late for almost every meeting on his calendar, if he showed up at all. This was well known throughout the organization through senior leadership and was joked about on many occasions with numerous people. This leader could not handle being called out about their tardiness or absence from meetings and would lay into anyone who mentioned it.

Part of being a leader is also being human, and we are all not good at everything. If you have something you need to work on as a leader, ask for help and own the struggle, and your employees will see that asking for help and embracing a skeleton or two can enhance your team dynamic immensely.

STEP 2: RECOGNIZING THE SIGNS

Imagine you notice a team member slipping up at work, maybe missing deadlines or making small mistakes they usually wouldn't. What if you saw these slips not just as off days but as cries for help?

Often, it's easy to chalk up a bad day to just that—a bad day—and give someone the benefit of the doubt. We tend to avoid tough conversations to spare each other's feelings, but over time, this kindness can turn into a bigger issue if it's a sign of underlying problems.

Think about a common situation where a manager wants to fire an employee but hasn't discussed the issues with them.

If you're open to recognizing the subtle signs of someone struggling, these conversations become easier to handle, especially if you already have a strong relationship with your team. When you know your employees well, you can spot when something's off and address it before it becomes a bigger problem.

From a workplace engagement standpoint, the quality of relationships within the team is crucial. Not every strained relationship needs to end in change, and not every disengaged employee will become fully engaged.

I've been there myself—a high performer who wasn't fully engaged but still committed to improving how we all work together. It's important to remember that not every employee will be 100 percent engaged all the time, and that's okay. Not all relationships in the workplace will be perfect, but recognizing when someone needs support can make a significant difference in their performance and overall workplace morale.

STEP 3: CHALLENGE YOUR FRAME OF MIND

What does it cost to support a good employee through a tough period vs. the costs of losing them, the expense of hiring and training someone new, and the loss of valuable organizational knowledge?

Remember, replacing an employee can cost six to nine months of their salary, not to mention the impact on the team's morale and productivity.

So, start with yourself.

When you're dealing with an issue or an employee who seems to be underperforming, start by asking yourself: "What assumptions have I made about this situation or this person?" Remember, no one wakes up in the morning planning to make your day harder.

Have you talked to them yet? It's important to recognize that the way you see things might not be how they experience them.

Have you weighed the costs?

This perspective shift is crucial.

I once managed someone who had panic attacks, which I didn't fully understand at the time. I didn't understand why this team member couldn't manage her mental health issues during critical times like payroll processing.

It wasn't until my panic attack years later that I truly understood the overwhelming nature of such episodes. I hadn't been as supportive or understanding as I could have been because I didn't grasp what she was going through.

How about you?

Think back to a time when you weren't fully present at work because something in your life was off balance—whether it was good or bad. Reflect on what would have helped you then and consider how you can offer similar support to your employees now.

Also, think about what wouldn't have helped or what you would have preferred not to hear during such a vulnerable time.

STEP 4: ACKNOWLEDGE YOUR LIMITS

Here's something I wish I knew 25 years ago. It's crucial to recognize your boundaries when supporting others at work.

Why?

1. You can't solve someone else's problems.
2. While you might want to help, stepping in as a fixer isn't your role.
3. Your role is not to be a personal advisor.
4. While someone might be facing challenges, your focus is on guiding them to professional support rather than taking on their burden.
5. Everyone has their battles, and sometimes, they just need someone to hear them.

6. Empathy and compassion have limits. It's natural to feel overwhelmed if you're constantly empathizing with others' difficulties. Recognize when to step back.

7. Consider your well-being. If you're dealing with your own issues, you might not have the capacity to support others.

It's okay to prioritize your mental health.

Understand that you won't always catch every sign of trouble, and that's okay. Acknowledging your limits is a strength, not a weakness.

STEP 5: KNOW THE BENEFITS

Know the benefits provided by your employer: where to go to get assistance, what is offered, and how to access the care.

You will not have a benefit to support every problem for every person. You want to ensure the benefits you have are communicated and easy to access.

Remember that less than 20 percent of employees have a high understanding of their benefits.

Below is a small list of the things that could be happening in someone's life at any given time. As a leader or HR person, how do managers support their employees who are going through these issues?

- Anxiety
- Burnout
- Caregiver responsibilities

- Depression
- Divorce
- Domestic violence
- Infertility problems
- Loss of a loved one
- Marriage
- Menopause
- Mental illness
- Miscarriage
- Money trouble
- Parenting issues (i.e., not sleeping, children with special needs, trouble with daycare or before- and after-school care, etc.)
- Partner retiring
- Substance abuse support for employee or partner/child
- Suicidal ideation

If, as an HR professional, you don't know if or how to get someone to the help your organization has available, you can bet your managers don't either.

Don't leave the conversations to chance—or worse, avoidance. Get managers the tools to know where to send employees when they need support. We will dive a little deeper into the communication of benefits during a later phase of your R.E.S.E.T.

STEP 6: KEEPING THE CONNECTION STRONG

Your or your manager's support of their employee should not end at connecting them with help.

How can you further support your employees?

What follow-up schedule would be helpful for them? You don't want to pester or micromanage, but leave the door open for outreach.

You do not need to tread on anyone's privacy to follow up. Tell your employees you want to be sure they are getting the support they need, so you will reach out weekly (or another frequency agreed on) to touch base.

Show that you care and are concerned for your employees beyond just the work they do for the organization.

WHAT CAN MANAGER TRAINING LOOK LIKE?

Manager training starts with self-awareness training and could be a combined first or second step in assessing internal relationships.

The World Health Organization recognizes self-awareness as one of ten life skills that promote well-being across all cultures.

Here's a resource that enhances your employees' understanding of themselves and each other.

One of the best experiences I've had within an organization from a training and relationship-building perspective was when the organization brought in trainers to work department by department via personality profiles, starting with the top and working down throughout the organization to support team dynamics.

Going through this training with the team was very eye-opening and gave me so much insight into why others and I do what we do. I had never felt that close and understood by a group of people I worked with until then or since.

You realize other people do things not because of anything you're doing but because of how they process, see, and experience things.

I found I could stop looking at personality traits as a personal attack or insult. This new insight into team member dynamics turns relationships around and allows you to use each other's strengths and learn to compensate for each other's areas where more growth is needed.

FROM DISENGAGED TO PRODUCTIVE: TRANSFORMING YOUR WORKFORCE

During my first stint as an entrepreneur, I marveled at all the varieties of coaching. Having spent years in the corporate world, I never knew coaching support existed on the scale that it does and how many people are interested in coaching as a career.

My experience with group coaching back then was life-altering! I realized there were other people out there who had the same struggles—imposter syndrome, self-sabotage, negative self-talk—and we supported and cheered each other on.

This is not the typical atmosphere of a corporate workplace. If we choose to bring coaching to the workplace, people will be seen and heard more often. And they won't fall by the wayside (because their boss had too many deliverables to meet).

There are a couple of effective ways to bring the benefits of coaching to an organization.

1. Hire coaches to work alongside teams with managers to help support the entire group. This would be particularly effective when you have larger teams and managers without the time to dedicate to managing. This also provides another perspective on team dynamics and may catch issues that can be addressed quickly and effectively.
2. Implement a stand-alone mental health provider or wellness provider that brings coaching to their

platform. Not everyone needs a therapist, but everyone can benefit from a coach.

3. Provide aspects of coach training to your managers. When I did my WellCoaches training during the pandemic, I was amazed by the positive nature, the listening skills I acquired, and the ability to probe and ask powerful questions. This aspect of managing was not taught within my master's program for HR, and we're not yet seeing this as mainstream training for MBAs and business degrees.

COACHING AND/OR CONSULTING: WHAT TO USE AND WHEN

If you work in the corporate world, chances are that you've worked with consultants. Consultants have a very traditional role within organizations. Leaders bring consultants in for the strategies they deploy and the set of prescriptions they offer.

Coaching is a more supportive process for long-term growth.

The proverb, "teach a man to fish," emphasizes that teaching someone how to do something is more helpful in the long run than simply doing it for them.

Coaches bring a mindset of discovery, listening to you, playing an empowering role, and helping you work through your challenges.

Both consultants and coaches have roles within the business world. Determine when your organization would be served better by "teaching employees to fish," and bring coaches in as your go-to talent support, conflict resolution facilitator, and extra well-being support at specific levels.

Coaches are also another set of eyes and ears when there is more needed than just their skills to listen and explore and when a referral to a therapist could be necessary.

PERFORMANCE ANXIETY

There is a lot of pressure in the corporate world to perform. When an organization's focus revolves heavily around performance and profit, managers may not see compassion and empathy as possible solutions or skills to be recognized and rewarded.

Giving your managers the opportunity to be more effective and empathic with their employees by giving them tools they may never have been exposed to increases manager engagement. Then, they will have more confidence in their one-on-one conversations and feel prepared for something unexpected.

A TOOL YOU CAN USE TODAY

Giving your managers the opportunity to be more effective and empathic with their employees by giving them tools they may never have been exposed to increases manager engagement. Then, they will have more confidence in their one-on-one conversations and feel prepared for something unexpected.

One little hinge that swings big doors in organizations is navigating difficult conversations.

If you're ready for some support, feel free to reach out to me for a conversation at dawn@dawnellery.com or linkedin.com/in/dawnellery. I look forward to meeting you!

TRANSFORMING THE TOXIC WORKPLACE

Navigating the complexities of a toxic workplace can feel isolating and deeply personal. Contrary to popular belief, a toxic boss isn't always the cause. Yet, with or without the boss, negative impacts can be concealed in the workplace, just like in personal relationships. We often excel at maintaining a facade that everything is fine, hiding the underlying tensions.

My firsthand experience of this began early in my HR career. In the beginning, my focus was on mastering the job and managing my tasks, leaving me oblivious to the toll it was taking on my health. It wasn't until I began recognizing symptoms of disengagement, depression, and burnout that I started questioning why I couldn't find a healthier work environment.

Like repeated, toxic relationships for some people, I kept finding my way back to toxic workplaces.

In these professional settings, I found myself replicating the unhealthy dynamics of my childhood. Much of my career was involved in total rewards—managing benefits, HR systems, compensation, payroll, wellness, and retirement systems—where perfection was not just expected but demanded.

Errors, despite being human, were never acknowledged, leaving no room for appreciation of our hard work.

This relentless pursuit of perfection was familiar to me; it mirrored the high standards and emotional trauma associated with failure I had experienced in both academics and sports during my upbringing.

At work, I acted as a mediator between my team and our superiors, shielding them from the brunt of any toxic behavior—a role not unfamiliar to me as a middle child in my family.

SURVIVING HR AS AN EMPATH

This realization of my high level of empathy and how it adversely affected my work environment was eye-opening. Despite my natural inclination to believe the best in others, I had to face the fact that I was drawn to the familiarity of these toxic environments, not because they were healthy but because they felt comfortable.

The pivotal moment came when I stepped away from corporate HR and took the leap as an entrepreneur. This period allowed me to work on personal growth and self-awareness, realizing that returning to the traditional HR role no longer suited me.

The rigid, analytical persona I had adopted in corporate life clashed with the more genuine, self-aware individual I had become.

That's why I created the R.E.S.E.T.

Awareness of toxicity and its causes is critical for any company. Toxicity can easily stem from negative interactions between managers and employees and may not always be visible to other leaders within the organization.

As you turn the pages, you'll discover how understanding and addressing these dynamics can foster a sense of belonging and growth, moving beyond traditional views and limitations of HR. This understanding is vital, not just for personal well-being but for cultivating a healthier, more inclusive workplace.

Actions and Reflections

- Take an honest look around you, your team, and your organization. How would you rate the relationships?
- If you asked employees if they have healthy relationships with their bosses and coworkers, how many would say yes, and how many would you trust were being honest?
- Do your managers have access to the tools they need to help their employees? If the answer is no or maybe and not a resounding *yes*, what resources can you pull together to support them?

A Tool You Can Use Today

Giving your managers the opportunity to be more effective and empathic with their employees by giving them tools they may never have been exposed to increases manager engagement. Then, they will have more confidence in their one-on-one conversations and feel prepared for something unexpected.

One little hinge that swings big doors in organizations is navigating difficult conversations.

If you're ready for some support, feel free to reach out to me for a conversation at dawn@dawnellery.com or linkedin.com/in/dawnellery. I look forward to meeting you!

What are your thoughts and insights?

_____

_____

_____

_____

_____

_____

_____

_____

_____

_____

_____

_____

_____

_____

R.E.S.E.T. Factor 2 – Envision: Reimagining HR

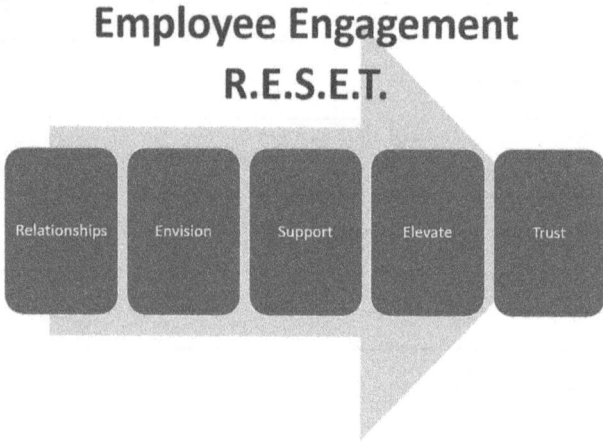

Employee Engagement R.E.S.E.T.

Relationships · Envision · Support · Elevate · Trust

Summary

Employees need to feel that they are growing both personally and professionally. Opportunities for development and advancement are crucial. Equally important is a sense of belonging. Employees should feel that they are an integral part of the organization and that their contributions are valued. Loneliness is a silent killer, more pervasive and insidious than ever before.

Envisioning HR as the team dedicated to fostering employee belonging transforms its role from traditional oversight to one of empowerment and support. When HR is focused on creating an inclusive environment, employees feel truly valued, respected, and seen for their unique contributions.

HR can drive initiatives that celebrate diversity, promote open dialogue, and support mental well-being, all of which enhance the sense of belonging and shared purpose within the workplace. By building a culture of belonging, HR helps employees feel connected and committed to the company's mission, ultimately boosting engagement, reducing turnover, and laying the groundwork for a resilient and high-performing organization.

Growth and True Belonging

We all want to belong.

Growth and belonging are the second foundation of any organization.

Psychologists equate our need for belonging with our need for love, highlighting its universal and fundamental nature. Prioritizing this will engage most, if not all, of your workforce.

Fostering diverse, equitable, and inclusive communities within organizations hinges on two critical elements: belonging and, as a result, growth. Growth needs to entail the aspiration to improve and develop personally, while belonging underscores the importance of nurturing a culture that celebrates diversity and anticipates positive transformation through those differences.

The current thought leadership around belonging has led to DE&I departments growing from HR departments and falling short on their goals and impact for several reasons.

Navigating Modern Challenges and Expanding Roles

Over the past few decades, HR has been tasked with managing an increasingly broad range of responsibilities, often dealing with an overwhelming workload. Close to half of HR leaders report not having enough staff since the increase in demands on their department from the pandemic.

Traditionally, HR's primary focus has been on mitigating company risk; this has attracted individuals whose skills align with this objective and who meet senior leadership's needs.

Coupled with smaller staff sizes and burnout among professionals who are frequently viewed merely as a cost center, this has created a recipe for disaster.

HR has been increasingly tasked with managing the fallout, support, and Q&As from numerous global and local disasters, illnesses, and events. The scope of HR responsibilities has expanded significantly, yet the size of HR teams typically has not kept pace.

However, in recent years, HR's role has broadened to include diversity, well-being, and employee engagement. Many current HR leaders are not adequately equipped to pivot and successfully manage these new responsibilities. As a result, HR has been set up to fail on several fronts.

With a change in expectations comes the need for new perspectives, out-of-the-box thinking, and envisioning what can be within organizations when we shift from managing to the lowest common denominator to managing to the highest potential or leading with high expectations.

This approach involves setting ambitious standards, encouraging growth, and empowering employees to reach their full capabilities as individuals. Instead of focusing on basic compliance or minimum performance levels, it prioritizes excellence, innovation, and individual strengths.

By fostering a culture where everyone is encouraged to strive for their best, this style of management can elevate overall performance, boost morale, and inspire a shared commitment to high standards across the organization.

DIVERSITY VS. BELONGING

Certain aspects of diversity can be tracked, analyzed, and targeted with specific goals, while others cannot. That's why I move beyond the concept of diversity. While I recognize its importance, I focus on fostering a sense of belonging.

Different personality traits often emerge when an organization shifts its focus toward happiness and belonging. It's essential to seek individuals with diverse skills to lead this change and introduce a fresh perspective on the value and importance of employees. These individuals can spearhead a new approach to leadership and effectively implement the organization's plans.

EMBRACING TRUE BELONGING

I prefer to use the term "belonging" rather than "diversity" for a reason. While diversity should be a given in today's world, it often isn't. Just as the pandemic forced companies to adopt remote work and greater flexibility, social inequity has pushed the corporate world to embrace diversity to recruit and retain talent.

I have never experienced disparity due to my race or ethnicity, but as a woman in the workplace, I have faced my share of sexism. My feelings of not fitting in and not belonging go much deeper than my gender and are invisible to most others. My severe bouts of depression went unnoticed. My thought processes and passion were often dismissed as either unwanted or too emotional, which had a lasting impact on me.

I had to hide, compromise, and suppress my compassion and empathy just to survive. Our approach to inclusion needs to evolve beyond surface-level diversity and grow to the point where there is no judgment.

When we begin from a place of no judgment, there's awareness, taking responsibility, and moving forward from a smarter and more elevated perspective.

EXPERIENCING THE POSITIVE: A CHANCE FOR REFLECTION

How do you see, take, feel, and experience someone at work when they send you emails, make suggestions, or provide feedback? Does your mind immediately go to all the ways this person might try to sabotage, undermine, or set you up? This can be common in work environments where employees are pitted against one another instead of working as a team for the benefit of all.

Not until I found a healthy work environment did a telltale sign of toxic environments become so apparent.

If you assume everyone is doing their best and working to support the organization and other employees within their departments, you will see interactions as positive. You will see the motivations of others as positive.

If the culture of your organization:

- Is one of a fear of failure
- Does not hold employees to the company values
- Always needs someone to be in the wrong, and they are called out and punished
- Supports managers blindsiding employees during performance reviews

What are your thoughts and insights?

_____

_____

_____

_____

_____

_____

_____

_____

_____

_____

_____

_____

_____

_____

_____

_____

R.E.S.E.T. FACTOR 3 – SUPPORT: COMPENSATION WON'T SOLVE FOR ENGAGEMENT

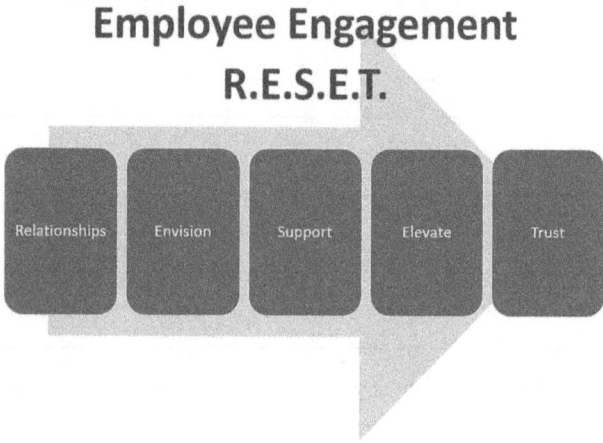

Employee Engagement
R.E.S.E.T.

Relationships | Envision | Support | Elevate | Trust

SUMMARY

It's time to shift your thinking from what an employer can offer you to how you will feel working for that employer. Yes, compensation and benefits are important, but they are not the only factors that contribute to employee well-being and engagement levels. A holistic approach to well-being includes physical, mental, financial, and emotional health.

Organizations that successfully provide support and resources that address all aspects of an employee's well-being are shown to prosper through happier employees, increased production and innovation, and reduced leave and burnout while contributing to increased customer retention and higher profits. Total rewards and well-being is the fourth step in creating a foundational level for an organization.

The term total rewards creates an expectation that you are thinking of the full package of compensation, benefits, and perks provided by an organization for their employees.

When I think about how we currently present the value of someone's employment in the corporate world, you typically see three buckets:

1. Cash: Annual salary or hourly rate, bonuses, and incentives
2. Benefits: Translated into dollars spent by the company for the benefit of the employee and their family for medical, dental, 401k match, commuter contribution, etc. (This list can vary in length and dollar amount.)
3. Perks that can be monetized: Like a free gym membership, food, snacks, coffee, or onsite meals.

We already know that 83 percent of people would take a pay cut to be happier at work. Yet the status quo places such an intense focus on pure compensation: someone's salary, bonus, and possibly incentives.

If so many people would be willing to work for less money to be happier, why do we keep trying to solve engagement with just compensation? Why don't you try to show them how they will feel working for you?

As the next step in your Employee Engagement R.E.S.E.T., move the strategy of total rewards beyond compensation and traditional benefits. Move beyond your total compensation statements to something that looks more like a total holistic well-being package, which I'll explain more about below.

I (as an employee) want to know how I will feel when I come to work for your company. Paint me that picture.

How to Create a Magnetic Brand that Attracts Top Talent and Makes Your Workplace a Beacon for High Performers

When you step into a new role at a company, imagine being greeted with an open invitation: "You are not expected to know everything walking in the door to our organization. You are invited to learn from those around you, share your knowledge with them, and collaborate to benefit all."

This approach isn't just a lofty ideal; it's a fundamental philosophy I'd love to see resonating through every level of a company. It sets the tone that learning is ongoing and collaborative, a stark contrast to the siloed and often isolating environments many experience in corporate settings.

In the entrepreneurial world, acknowledging that no one is infallible and that everyone has room to grow is standard. This mindset fosters an environment where the pressure to appear perfect doesn't overshadow the more critical goal of growth and improvement.

Think about it: When new hires step into a role, they're typically bombarded with the pressures of "proving themselves" within the first 30, 60, or 90 days.

Many companies perform performance reviews after 60 or 90 days.

What if, instead, the company also had to demonstrate its commitment to supporting that new hire? A reciprocal review process where the employee's performance and the organization's support systems are evaluated could transform the typical workplace dynamic.

Reflecting on my transition from corporate HR to entrepreneurship highlighted a stark disparity. In my businesses, it is normal—expected, even—to admit shortcomings and work actively with coaches to address them.

This open acknowledgment that everyone is a work in progress was liberating and constructive. However, in many traditional corporate roles, admitting to struggles or areas for improvement is often seen as a weakness, something to mask or hide rather than address head-on.

THE ROLE OF LEADERSHIP IN FOSTERING A HEALTHY WORK ENVIRONMENT

The truth is that an organization thrives when its leaders and structure actively support every employee's growth. This support can mean coaching, yes, but it also embraces the idea that learning is ongoing and mistakes are part of the journey.

When employees feel safe to admit their challenges without fear of retribution, they are more likely to seek help and less likely to feel isolated with their problems. This kind of supportive environment not only increases employee engagement but also loyalty and productivity.

Employees being able to see their leaders as real people who make mistakes, own them, and learn from them is invaluable.

Ultimately, fostering a culture where employees are encouraged to be their whole selves, acknowledging both strengths and areas needing improvement, isn't just good ethics; it's good business. By adopting a more humane approach to employee development—one that recognizes the value of learning and growing from mistakes—you cultivate a more resilient and adaptable organization. In such a culture, employees don't just survive; they thrive, and so does the business.

IT'S NOT WOO-WOO: SCARCITY VS. ABUNDANCE AND SEEING THE WORLD DIFFERENTLY

In most of the corporate world, the prevailing mindset is one of scarcity. This pervasive belief that there is never enough—be it resources, talent, or opportunities—fosters a competitive atmosphere where companies vie relentlessly for the best, as dictated by ever-shifting market demands and economic currents.

This scarcity mindset not only fuels the recruitment wars but also influences the power dynamics between employers and potential employees, with each side negotiating from a perceived lack of options.

Contrast this with the entrepreneurial approach, where abundance thinking prevails. Entrepreneurs are coached to view the world through a lens of possibility and plenty. Instead of focusing on limitations, they see opportunities for collaboration and innovation.

Abundance thinking isn't just about being optimistic; it's about recognizing the vast potential that exists and leveraging it for creative and strategic gains. This mindset encourages seeing the glass as half full, fostering a culture of gratitude, and recognizing the myriad opportunities surrounding us.

This shift in perspective can profoundly impact how businesses operate and compete. For instance, in the entrepreneurial realm, the concept of competition transforms into collaboration. Entrepreneurs often find that by partnering with others in the same niche, they can enhance their offerings and expand their reach, effectively growing the pie rather than fighting over the existing slices.

This approach acknowledges that by sharing knowledge and resources, businesses can achieve more together than they could alone.

However, the transition to abundance thinking in the corporate sector is gradual and fraught with challenges. CEOs and business leaders are beginning to recognize the need for a shift toward more sustainable and health-oriented business practices, but old habits die hard. The traditional scarcity mindset has deep roots, reinforced by institutional norms and economic structures that prioritize short-term gains over long-term well-being.

A common example of prioritizing short-term gains over long-term well-being is when an employee who has clearly behaved in a way that an average employee would be fired for is kept and has no repercussions due to their client base or the sales they are bringing in.

Leaving inappropriate or disruptive and unhealthy behavior unrecognized, unacknowledged, and without repercussions potentially impacts the mental health of other employees.

To truly embrace abundance, corporate leaders must start by reevaluating their strategies from the ground up. It involves cultivating a workplace environment that values employee well-being, encourages innovation, and embraces flexibility—traits that are naturally ingrained in entrepreneurial settings.

By adopting this mindset, companies not only enhance their competitiveness but also contribute to a healthier, more productive business ecosystem that can thrive amidst changes and challenges.

Embracing an abundance mindset doesn't mean ignoring the realities of business pressures; rather, it's about changing the approach to these challenges from one of limitation to one of possibilities. This shift could lead to a more fulfilled workforce, more innovative problem-solving, and, ultimately, a more successful and resilient business.

YOUR EMPLOYEE IS A WHOLE PERSON, NOT JUST A WORKER

While you conceptually know that when someone shows up for work, they still have their whole life taking place at the same time. There isn't always the space and flexibility for these competing priorities. Work has to be done, reports created, presentations made, and sales closed. The conflict comes because your problems don't stop at the office door, appointments don't make themselves, and parents, partners, and children have needs that don't always wait for 5:00 p.m.

We've become so good at acting like everything is okay that it's now hard for people to know when someone is going through something that could be impacting their health and performance.

People act as if everything is okay at work even though it's not for many different reasons:

- They are private and don't want anyone to know.
- They are ashamed or embarrassed.
- They're afraid of their manager finding out.
- They're afraid of getting fired.
- They don't want to put work on others.

When people act okay, it doesn't make everything okay because distraction, stress, and anxiety all lead to burnout, disengagement, unhealthy habits, increased medical claims, and low productivity.

Let's look at ways to bring the whole person to work.

Challenging Groupthink: Risks of Maintaining the Status Quo

Groupthink is a pervasive mindset that stifles innovation and individuality. Sadly, you'll find it in most organizations, and it prioritizes conformity and harmony over independent thinking and robust debate. It's a phenomenon where the fear of conflict and desire for cohesiveness lead teams to make irrational decisions, often at the cost of creativity and effectiveness. You've likely seen it yourself: the push for uniformity, the avoidance of dissent, and the suppression of new ideas.

Groupthink: Squirrel!

This environment fosters what's known as "shiny object syndrome," a focus on the latest trend or problem that promises to be the quick fix to deep-seated issues within the organization. Like magpies attracted to shiny objects, companies chase after new concepts or technologies, hoping they will magically resolve all their challenges.

However, this often leads to a cycle of enthusiasm and disillusionment as the underlying issues, such as childcare, paid maternity leave, and adequate retirement savings, remain unaddressed. These are not just minor problems but significant concerns that affect employee retention and satisfaction.

GROUPTHINK: MENTAL HEALTH

For example, consider the issue of mental health in the workplace. During the pandemic, mental health emerged as a critical concern. Companies started to pay attention, but many treated it as just another box to check—providing minimal support through employee assistance programs (EAPs) that are underutilized.

The reality is that effective mental health support requires more than just an EAP; it needs a comprehensive approach that integrates mental health into the overall wellness strategy of the company.

GROUPTHINK: COMPENSATION

Furthermore, let's talk about compensation practices. At a recent HR conference, a revealing moment came when a presenter from a major consulting firm highlighted how the expected salary increases are always around the average of 3 percent.

When the audience, composed of HR professionals and leaders from various companies, was asked about their planned increases, nearly everyone confirmed they were sticking to this average. The presenter pointed out that this perpetuates the status quo because companies continue to report similar figures.

This moment of candidness from the presenter underscored how deeply entrenched these practices are and how they contribute to a cycle of conformity that hinders real progress.

In essence, the corporate world needs a paradigm shift from scarcity to abundance, from groupthink to individual empowerment, and from short-term fixes to long-term solutions.

Only by acknowledging and addressing these deep-rooted issues with honesty and strategic focus can businesses hope to foster a truly innovative and supportive workplace culture. It's about looking beyond the immediate and superficial to make changes that genuinely enhance the work environment and the lives of those within it.

This is not just beneficial for the employees but is also crucial for the long-term success and resilience of the organization.

A TOOL YOU CAN USE TODAY

Giving your managers the opportunity to be more effective and empathic with their employees by giving them tools they may never have been exposed to increases manager engagement. Then, they will have more confidence in their one-on-one conversations and feel prepared for something unexpected.

One little hinge that swings big doors in organizations is navigating difficult conversations.

If you're ready for some support, feel free to reach out to me for a conversation at dawn@dawnellery.com or linkedin.com/in/dawnellery. I look forward to meeting you!

What are your thoughts and insights?

_____

_____

_____

_____

_____

_____

_____

_____

_____

_____

_____

_____

_____

_____

R.E.S.E.T. Factor 4 – ELEVATE: Profit by Putting People First

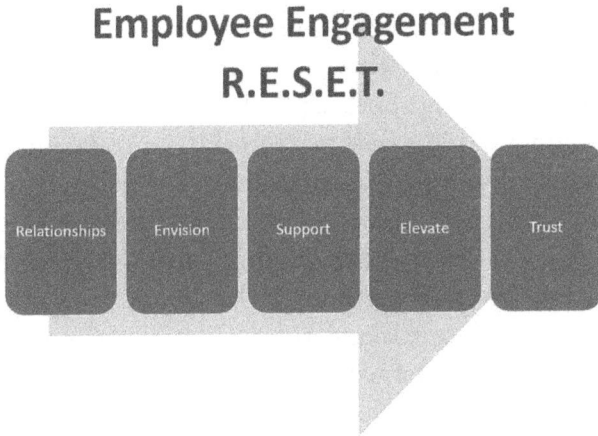

Employee Engagement R.E.S.E.T.

Relationships	Envision	Support	Elevate	Trust

Summary

The values, mission, and goals of the company should align with those of its employees. Employees who feel that their work is meaningful and contributes to a larger purpose are more likely to be engaged and committed to the organization.

In the pursuit of long-term success, aligning the well-being of employees with the strategic goals of an organization isn't just a "nice to have;" it's essential for sustainable growth and profitability. Companies that truly put people first recognize that alignment, purpose, and engagement are not only mutually supportive but also powerful drivers of profitability. Organizations create a workplace where purpose and productivity thrive side-by-side by prioritizing employees' needs and aligning them with the company's mission.

Engagement naturally increases when employees feel their roles have a purpose and are connected to broader goals. This sense of purpose transforms how individuals approach their work: Tasks become meaningful, ideas flow more freely, and collaboration strengthens. An engaged workforce is an invaluable asset, leading to higher retention rates, reduced turnover costs, and increased innovation. Employees become invested partners in the company's success, contributing to a foundation that supports not only people but also robust profitability.

This chapter explores the vital connection between a people-first approach and financial performance, demonstrating that companies built on principles of alignment and purpose don't just survive; they lead.

From Toxic to Profit

In many organizations, the approach to creating leadership structures, policies, and culture often lacks consideration for the actual needs of the employees.

Driven by a fear of legal repercussions, companies tend to design policies that cater to the lowest common denominator, inadvertently creating overly rigid and restrictive environments. This overcautious approach can directly contribute to employee disengagement and poor well-being.

The term "toxic work environment" has evolved significantly since the 1960s. Originally used to describe workplaces that posed physical health risks due to actual toxic substances, it now often refers to environments that cause emotional and mental strain, which can also lead to physical health issues.

This shift highlights a growing recognition of the profound impact that workplace atmospheres can have on an individual's health and well-being.

By addressing these pain points within the workplace, you can significantly enhance employee engagement and overall well-being. It's crucial for businesses to rethink how they implement policies and structures to foster a more supportive and healthy work environment.

People First and Profiting (At the Same Time)

When the initial shock of the pandemic subsided, many people found themselves working in their homes.

People managers and leadership were pleasantly surprised that teams were extremely productive even with the short notice of shifting to 100 percent virtual and with the state of the health of the world. Flexibility and working from home were forced on the corporate world, and people rose to the challenge.

People have not always been given the opportunity to rise to a challenge within the corporate world. Instead, change in the corporate world is typically slow and cautious until it becomes forced and legislated.

Let's look at a couple of examples of changes in the workplace and how long they've taken.

Example #1 Paid Maternity Leave

This example underscores the slow pace of change, particularly evident in the absence of federal paid maternity leave, with only three states (CA, RI, NJ) currently implementing active policies.

Twenty-five percent of women are compelled to return to work within just two weeks of giving birth to provide for their families. Additionally, a staggering 40 percent of women do not qualify for the Family Medical Leave Act (FMLA), which offers 12 weeks of job-protected leave. Furthermore, a mere 12 percent of women in the private sector have access to any form of paid maternity leave.

It's noteworthy that the United States stands alone among high-income countries in lacking federal paid maternity leave, with 178 other nations guaranteeing such benefits.

This serves as a poignant example of necessary but neglected change, where profits have taken precedence over the well-being of individuals.

However, there's been a positive trend in the past five to ten years, with a growing emphasis on diversity leading to advancements in parental leave policies. This not only benefits birth mothers but also spouses, partners, and adoptive parents, providing paid time off dedicated to new parents.

Nevertheless, as more companies insist on employees returning to physical work locations, we're witnessing a decline in the number of women in the workforce once again.

Example #2 Casual Dress in the Workplace

When I entered the corporate world in the 1990s, there was a strict expectation for business attire: suits for men and either suits or at least pants and jackets for women. However, there was a growing demand from employees for more casual dress codes.

Employees argued that casual attire would not only save money but also increase productivity by fostering a more comfortable work environment. Initially, corporate conferences featured a plethora of indistinguishable dress styles, requiring specific definitions such as "business casual," "business casual evening," and "sporty business casual."

Despite the gradual adoption of more relaxed dress codes, the prevailing corporate belief remained rooted in the notion that one's appearance directly correlated with professional competence. There was a common assumption among corporate leaders that allowing employees to dress casually would result in decreased productivity, disrespect toward clients, or reduced engagement solely based on attire.

However, as some companies began to embrace casual dress in the workplace, dress codes became a competitive advantage in recruitment. Leaders recognized the potential to attract and retain talent by offering business casual attire as a perk.

In the financial sector, where I worked in 2016, the promise of jeans on Fridays was used as an incentive to encourage desired behavior among employees. For instance, if a certain percentage of employees agreed to a new handbook or completed mandatory training, they would earn the privilege of wearing jeans on a specified Friday.

This strategy proved effective for both retention and recruitment, leading to widespread adoption across industries. However, while the "everybody's doing it" mentality may drive change, it should not be the sole reason for businesses to innovate around employee well-being, support, comfort, or flexibility. The mere popularity of a practice should not justify its continuation if it fails to serve the best interests of employees.

LEAD THE CHARGE IN REVOLUTIONIZING WORKPLACE WELL-BEING

Increased flexibility in where and when people work has been requested by employees for decades, just like the two examples above. Reasons behind the desire for more flexibility vary by person and their needs, but even after tests were performed and results showed increased performance with greater flexibility, the corporate world would not move the needle on flexibility of where and when employees work in a significant way until it was forced to by the pandemic.

If you are going to move forward in creating a culture of engagement and well-being, it will take doing what hasn't been done before.

You got this.

Don't Make Work More Difficult

This book is about increasing employee engagement in ways that fall outside of your traditional rewards and recognition programs. Reward and recognition programs will do no good if your policies and procedures are draining your employees daily.

Let's look at three pain points that are common to most of us who work outside of the home and what you can do to reduce the pain and increase engagement and productivity:

How easy or how frustrating does your company make someone's day?

Navigating the Shift from Toxic Work Environments to Thriving Spaces

What are some of the common feelings or behavioral outcomes (physiologically) when you get frustrated?

- Anger
- Stress and depression
- Irritability and aggressive behavior
- Loss of confidence
- A generally positive person turns into a person who sees nearly everything as a problem

None of the above outcomes are something you would pay to achieve within an organization you are leading. By having frustrating processes and procedures in place—whether you are aware of them or not—the above feelings and behaviors are almost guaranteed to crop up daily, increasing frustration and decreasing engagement and productivity.

Find out what makes your employees' jobs more difficult or frustrating.

Ask yourself:

When do you feel the most frustrated at work?

What are the things that get in the way of you being productive?

These are pain points within your organization, and if you can solve some of these, you can expect an automatic increase in the engagement levels of your employees, plus less stress and frustration, which snowballs to better well-being.

Chances are good that you won't need to look very hard for some of these pain points. These exist at different places and levels of employees within every organization. Here are some of the places to look:

- Processes that are integral to your organization's day-to-day operations
- Administrative tasks that make work or data flow
- How easy is it for changes to be made to current processes?
- How receptive and ready are your support departments to receive feedback on processes?
- How receptive is leadership to new and different ideas?

IT TAKES A (CORPORATE) VILLAGE

If you want to solve problems in your organization, you can't rely on just one department (or individual) to do it. That means issues shouldn't be confined to specific departments like IT or HR and shouldn't be addressed solely by executives because executives are often insulated from many operational hiccups by layers of support that most employees don't have. This detachment can lead to a lack of awareness about the daily challenges employees face, challenges that are directly tied to the efficiency and morale of the workforce.

For instance, consider the structure of your corporate departments. Departments like HR and IT are integral to the daily operations of a company and interact with all employees. Consequently, they are often central to the creation of systemic pain points. For example, a common issue arises with time-tracking systems. In one organization I worked with, hourly employees had to enter their work hours into three different systems. This redundant process was time-consuming and led to payroll errors and billing issues, affecting a wide range of stakeholders.

This issue persisted because it became a norm; no one questioned it seriously enough to initiate change. It was only when a new billing system was implemented and the term "timecards" was used that the leadership realized the extent of the issue. This revelation led to the formation of a task force aimed at consolidating these systems into a single, more efficient process.

Another personal example highlights the assumptions about knowledge and responsibility in specialized roles like HR. Despite being an experienced HR manager, I often find myself struggling with outdated hiring processes when I need to recruit new team members. The assumption that HR professionals are omniscient about all aspects of human resources can lead to significant inefficiencies and personal stress.

Furthermore, workplace policies regarding time off and the cultural norms around disconnecting from work significantly impact employee well-being. Despite what policies might dictate, the real test of their effectiveness lies in their implementation. Leaders and managers play a crucial role in this. They must not only preach the importance of taking breaks but also practice it themselves to avoid a culture of constant availability that leads to burnout.

TURNING THE TIDE ON EMPLOYEE DISENGAGEMENT WITH PROVEN STRATEGIES

First, it has to start with leadership because if they're not on board, nobody else will be. From there, the most effective approach is holistic, including input from all levels of an organization. It involves recognizing the interconnectedness of systems and policies and the way they impact the day-to-day experiences of employees.

It's only through comprehensive understanding and effort that real improvements in engagement and well-being can happen.

A Tool You Can Use Today

Giving your managers the opportunity to be more effective and empathic with their employees by giving them tools they may never have been exposed to increases manager engagement. Then, they will have more confidence in their one-on-one conversations and feel prepared for something unexpected.

One little hinge that swings big doors in organizations is navigating difficult conversations.

If you're ready for some support, feel free to reach out to me for a conversation at dawn@dawnellery.com or linkedin.com/in/dawnellery. I look forward to meeting you!

What are your thoughts and insights?

_____
_____
_____
_____
_____
_____
_____
_____
_____
_____
_____
_____
_____
_____

R.E.S.E.T. Factor 5 – Trust: Communication and Innovation that Transform

**Employee Engagement
R.E.S.E.T.**

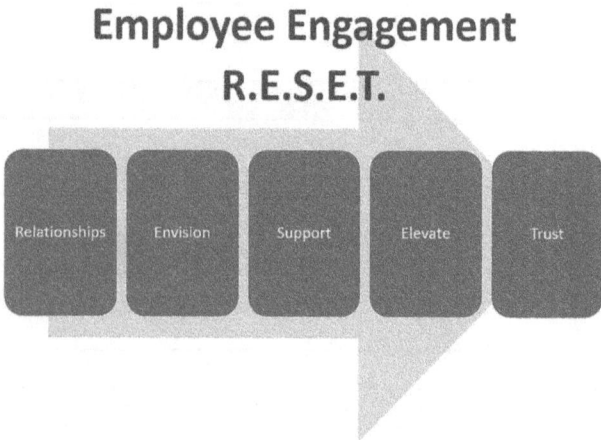

Summary

Communication weaves through any organization or relationship and can lead to positive experiences or soul-crushing despair; it could be the reason your project failed, the filing didn't happen on time, or someone didn't get paid. The disbursement of information in many organizations suffers from needing to move through too many filters and typically goes in one direction: down.

Good communication is the backbone of a thriving workplace, impacting profitability, engagement, and employee well-being in powerful ways. When communication flows openly and effortlessly, employees feel informed, valued, and connected to the company's mission, which enhances engagement and loyalty. Clear communication reduces misunderstandings, fosters collaboration, and speeds up problem-solving, all of which boost productivity and reduce costly errors. Additionally, a culture of open dialogue supports mental well-being, as employees feel safe expressing concerns and sharing ideas. By cultivating effective communication, companies not only strengthen trust but also lay the groundwork for sustainable profitability and a healthy, engaged workforce.

INFORMATION EXCHANGE

In any organization, the flow and management of communication—or, as I prefer to call it, information exchange—can make or break your success. This is like a two-way street: Information should not only come from the top, but it should also travel upwards, allowing every segment of the company to voice feedback effectively.

Yet, too often, the reality mirrors the children's game of "telephone," where the original message mutates beyond recognition as it whispers down the line.

Ineffective communication costs organizations $2 trillion per year in lost productivity.

What begins as a crucial corporate directive can end up as distorted versions that bear little resemblance to their original intentions, often stripped of their urgency or altered in tone—not to mention the employee feedback that never quite makes it back up the ladder.

Moreover, silence in the workplace can be misinterpreted as agreement or consent, which is a dangerous assumption to make. In many cases, when individuals do not voice objections or concerns, it is not because they agree with the decisions being made but because they feel powerless to affect any change. This silence should not be mistaken for acceptance but recognized as a sign that not all is well.

As a leader, if you notice silence around you, see it not as a confirmation that your team is on board but as a signal that something deeper may need addressing.

TRANSFORMING YOUR WORKPLACE THROUGH COMMUNICATION AND INNOVATIVE EMPLOYEE ENGAGEMENT STRATEGIES

Effective communication about workplace benefits is a persistent challenge in many organizations, often resulting in employees not fully understanding or utilizing the benefits available to them. This difficulty stems from several factors, including the complexity of benefits packages, insufficient or unclear communication from employers, and employees' varying levels of financial literacy and interest.

Benefits packages can be intricate, encompassing health insurance, retirement plans, wellness programs, and other perks, each with its own set of rules, options, and implications. This complexity can overwhelm employees, particularly if the information is not presented in a straightforward and accessible manner.

One major issue is the lack of clarity and consistency in how benefits information is communicated. Often, information about benefits is dispersed through multiple channels, such as emails, intranet sites, brochures, and meetings, which can lead to inconsistencies and confusion.

When these communications are full of technical jargon or legalistic language, employees may struggle to comprehend the details and make informed decisions. Moreover, the timing of these communications is crucial; information shared during onboarding may be quickly forgotten, while consistent updates are necessary to keep employees informed about any changes or new options that typically don't make the to-do list.

Furthermore, the diverse needs and preferences of the workforce add another layer of complexity to communicating benefits. Employees at different stages of their careers and with varying personal circumstances will prioritize different aspects of their benefits packages.

For instance, younger employees might be more interested in student loan repayment assistance or career development opportunities, while older employees may focus on retirement planning and health benefits. Tailoring communication to address these varied interests can be challenging but is essential for ensuring all employees understand and appreciate the full value of their benefits.

The lack of effective communication about benefits can lead to significant disadvantages for both employees and employers. Employees may miss out on valuable benefits that could enhance their well-being and financial security, leading to dissatisfaction and reduced engagement. This can translate to higher turnover rates, lower productivity, and increased healthcare and administrative costs for employers.

Improving the clarity, consistency, and personalization of benefits communication is vital. When employers put effort and planning into leveraging a mix of communication methods, such as interactive webinars, personalized benefits statements, and one-on-one consultations, it ensures employees fully understand and can effectively utilize their workplace benefits.

HOLISTIC TOTAL REWARDS

I talked earlier about moving toward holistic total rewards and away from the more traditional compensation and benefits you use today to help employees understand the value of the employer's contribution to their lives.

Creating an environment, a process, and a communication strategy for employees that conveys more than just the compensation you pay or the traditional benefits you provide is critical to how they feel about working at your company.

When an employee leaves their job and has to pay for benefits through COBRA, this is typically the first time they fully appreciate the value of their employer's contribution to their benefits; it's the same concept as how you want them to feel while working with you.

You communicate this feeling of belonging and support while people are working for you, so there is appreciation and understanding of the environment you've created. This can only be delivered by communication from leadership and marketing the experience.

The focus shifts from standard compensation and benefits to how my life improves and how I improve myself as a person.

The full embracement of the person coming into the workplace becomes the focus of their understanding of how you support them and their families.

DISCOVER THE REAL REASONS BEHIND YOUR EMPLOYEE TURNOVER

Avoiding difficult conversations is another common issue that plagues personal and professional interactions. People shy away from these talks for numerous reasons: fear of conflict, reluctance to cause discomfort, or simply not feeling prepared to tackle the issues at hand.

However, avoidance only leads to festering problems and, ultimately, greater dissatisfaction. Through my experience with Sweet Escape, especially around Valentine's Day, I realized how often people use gifts as a substitute for the conversations they need but avoid having. This avoidance strategy does not just apply to personal relationships but is rampant in professional settings as well.

In the workplace, instead of confronting the real issues—be it poor management relationships, ineffective processes, or merely an adherence to the status quo—companies often throw money at these problems, hoping for a quick fix.

This approach is akin to giving gifts instead of addressing the issues at hand; companies spend over $21 billion on corporate swag that will mostly end up in the donation pile. These tactics are superficial and rarely resolve the underlying difficulties. Real improvement requires open, honest dialogue and a willingness to tackle difficult topics head-on.

Finally, the information exchanged during the hiring or exit process can provide profound insights into the organization's true environment. The initial phases of employment can often feel like a honeymoon period, where every interaction is polished to perfection.

However, once the novelty wears off, the reality sets in, and sometimes, it's not what was promised. Likewise, when employees exit, particularly from a less-than-ideal environment, their parting words (or their choice to remain silent) can be very telling.

If we insist on maintaining professionalism to the extent that we never address the issues upon departure, we miss a crucial opportunity to rectify and improve the corporate culture. Through these honest exchanges, organizations can truly evolve and enhance their environments for everyone involved.

WRAPPING UP

As you reach these final pages, I extend my gratitude to you for joining this journey. Thank you for accompanying me on this exploration.

- I promised that if you've read this book, you will know how to start creating a better workplace by better understanding the root cause of disengagement in your pursuit of increasing engagement, retention, productivity, and well-being.
- I debunked the biggest myths HR currently relies on to attempt to increase organizational engagement and well-being. You now see the deeper drivers of disengagement and can start to address the root causes within your organization.
- You have been introduced to my framework for an Employee Engagement R.E.S.E.T. You can begin to see how these steps could come alive within your organization in a holistic manner and challenge the status quo. Your eyes have been opened to the crucial aspect of difficult conversations, and with the ABC

approach to managers identifying and supporting their employees, you can start to make a vital shift in resulting performance.

- You can now see how greater honesty and self-awareness can work in collaboration to support a healthy workplace. By seeing performance issues as a cry for help, you can help managers change their focus from punitive and potentially unnecessary performance management to facing difficult conversations at the moment that have a positive long-term impact on relationships.

- I've planted the idea of looking toward the entrepreneurial community and how support and authenticity strengthen the learning process and allow people to ask for help and how that would serve the corporate world. There is a way for both employees and employers to get what they need without sacrificing the employee.

- You've seen that enhancing employee engagement and well-being is not just a noble endeavor; it's a necessity for any organization aiming to thrive. Employee engagement and well-being are intertwined, with each influencing the other. Engagement is about employees feeling connected to their work and the organization's mission, while well-being encompasses their physical, mental, emotional, and financial health.

- You now know how to holistically support your employees down a healthier path that creates real engagement, well-being, productivity, and retention while potentially saving your organization from unnecessary programs and status-quo thinking.

Not to mention that you'll save thousands, millions, or even billions of dollars each year.

How does that sound?

A TOOL YOU CAN USE TODAY

Giving your managers the opportunity to be more effective and empathic with their employees by giving them tools they may never have been exposed to increases manager engagement. Then, they will have more confidence in their one-on-one conversations and feel prepared for something unexpected.

One little hinge that swings big doors in organizations is navigating difficult conversations.

If you're ready for some support, feel free to reach out to me for a conversation at dawn@dawnellery.com or linkedin.com/in/dawnellery. I look forward to meeting you!

LET'S HAVE A CHAT

If you're ready to elevate your organization, reach out to me today for a conversation at dawn@dawnellery.com or linkedin.com/in/dawnellery. I look forward to meeting you!

ACKNOWLEDGMENTS

I want to acknowledge and give hope to all those working in toxic environments, enduring trauma for a paycheck, wondering if it's you or them, and just barely making it through the workweek. There are healthy work environments out there—never stop looking. Remember, you are always so much more than what you do for a living.

For those pretending to be something you are not to earn your paycheck, take off your mask—even if it's only in private. Allow someone to see the authentic you.

For those who experienced childhood trauma, in whatever form it took, if you can face it and heal, I offer you the strength to achieve this. It may not be something you can move on from until you do.

For the one who wouldn't take the vow, you have been my sister all these years, Laura.

To my first wellness coach, Karen Brooks, you were the friend I desperately needed and the rock that held me in place for months as the ground crumbled beneath me. May you always be well and know the impact you had on my life.

To Ric, the mentor and friend who kept it together for me in the face of dire confessions, who initially suggested the safer path of a sex toy party business and, when I said that wasn't me, responded, "Then open the sex shop." Your ability to see me and coach me was life-changing.

To all the women who supported my entrepreneurial journey, showing me there were women who supported other women, had their backs, and even cheered the successes of others, you allowed me to see my struggles as normal and surmountable.

To those who were rays of light in the darkness—Diane, Marianne, Joe, Dorothy, Margie, Laura, and Terry—you are in my thoughts often.

The more recent additions to my life who have seen and supported my healing—my friends from mood school, Sharyl, Hillary, and Deo—your friendships mean the world to me.

Jackie Beno, I leaned on you and asked for help for the first time, and that is a credit to your gifts. I owe the completion of this work and my continued existence to you.

For the group brought together by Ben G., who acted as my lifeline during times of darkness, thank you for showing up and allowing me to be part of your journey. For Ben G., I thank you, from the bottom of my heart, for walking with me through the completion of this work with the hurdles, healing, and layers of the onion that just wouldn't stop peeling. You are a treasured gift to those who meet you.

And to those who taught the lessons it took me so long to learn, I give a special acknowledgment to you all. I would not be where I am, appreciate what I have, or have healed all I needed to heal without all of you.

While I know you were brought into my life for a reason, I am happy to have learned, healed, and moved forward.